THE
PASSI·
LIFE

BIBLE STUDY SERIES

MW00810792

Philippians

HEAVEN'S
JOY

8-WEEK STUDY GUIDE

BroadStreet
PUBLISHING

BroadStreet Publishing Group, LLC
Racine, Wisconsin, USA
BroadStreetPublishing.com

The Passionate Life Bible Study Series
PHILIPPIANS: HEAVEN'S JOY 8-WEEK STUDY GUIDE

Edited by Jeremy Bouma

ISBN-13: 978-1-4245-5331-0 (soft cover)
ISBN-13: 978-1-4245-5332-7 (e-book)

To purchase any of the study guides in the The Passionate Life Bible Study Series in bulk for use in groups, please send an email to orders@broadstreetpublishing.com.

Cover design by Chris Garborg at GarborgDesign.com
Typesetting by Katherine Lloyd at theDESKonline.com

Printed in the United States of America

16 17 18 19 20 5 4 3 2 1

Contents

Using The Passionate Life Bible Study 5

Introduction to Philippians 9

Lesson 1 **God's Grace—Gloriously Expressed, Faithfully Completed:**
Philippians 1:1–11.. 11

Lesson 2 **Our Chaos, God's Gospel Good:** Philippians 1:12–18........ 19

Lesson 3 **Christ Made Manifest, in Life or Death:** Philippians 1:19–30... 26

Lesson 4 **Let Jesus' Mind-Set Become Your Motivation:**
Philippians 2:1–11....................................... 36

Lesson 5 **Live a Joy-Filled, Faithful Life:** Philippians 2:12–30........... 45

Lesson 6 **Die with Christ to Live Again:** Philippians 3:1–11 52

Lesson 7 **Forget Your Past, Fasten Your Heart to the Future:**
Philippians 3:12–21...................................... 60

Lesson 8 **Always Be Cheerful with Joyous Celebration:**
Philippians 4:1–23....................................... 68

Using The Passionate Life Bible Study

The psalmist declares, "Truth's shining light guides me in my choices and decisions; the revelation of your Word makes my pathway clear" (Psalm 119:105).

This verse forms the foundation of The Passionate Life Bible Study series. Not only do we want to kindle within you a deep, burning passion for God and his Word, but we also want to let the Word's light blaze a bright path before you to help you make truth-filled choices and decisions, while encountering the heart of God along the way.

God longs to have his Word expressed in a way that unlocks the passion of his heart for the reader. Inspired by The Passion Translation but usable with any Bible translation, this is a heart-level Bible study, from the passion of God's heart to the passion of your heart. Our goal is to trigger inside you an over-whelming response to the truth of the Bible.

DISCOVER. EXPLORE. EXPERIENCE. SHARE.

Each of the following lessons is divided into four sections: *Discover the Heart of God*; *Explore the Heart of God*; *Experience the Heart of God*; and *Share the Heart of God*. They are meant to guide your study of the truth of God's Word, while drawing you closer and deeper into his passionate heart for you and your world.

The *Discover* section is designed to help you make observations about the reading. Every lesson opens with the same three questions: What did you notice, perhaps for the first time? What questions do you have? And, what did you learn about the heart of God? There are no right answers here! They are meant to jump-start your journey into God's truth by bringing to the surface your initial impressions about the passage. The other questions help draw your attention to specific points the author wrote and discover the truths God is conveying.

Explore takes you deeper into God's Word by inviting you to think more critically and explain what the passage is saying. Often there is some extra information to highlight and clarify certain aspects of the passage, while inviting you to make connections. Don't worry if the answers aren't immediately apparent. Sometimes you may need to dig a little deeper or take a little more time to think. You'll be grateful you did, because you will have tapped into God's revelation-light in greater measure!

Experience is meant to help you do just that: experience God's heart for you personally. It will help you live out God's Word by applying it to your unique life situation. Each question in this section is designed to bring the Bible into your world in fresh, exciting, and relevant ways. At the end of this section, you will have a better idea of how to make choices and decisions that please God, while walking through life on clear paths bathed in the light of his revelation!

The final section is *Share*. God's Word isn't meant to be merely studied or memorized; it's meant to be shared with other people—both through living and telling. This section helps you understand how the reading relates to growing closer to others, to enriching your fellowship and relationship with your world. It also helps you listen to the stories of those around you, so you can bridge Jesus' story with their stories.

SUGGESTIONS FOR INDIVIDUAL STUDY

Reading and studying the Bible is an exciting journey! This study is designed to help you encounter the heart of God and let his Word to you reach deep down into your very soul—all so you can live and enjoy the life he intends for you. And like with any journey, a number of practices will help you along the way:

1. Begin your lesson time in prayer, asking God to open up his Word to you in new ways, show areas of your heart that need teaching

and healing, and correct any area in which you're living contrary to his desires for your life.

2. Read the opening section to gain an understanding of the major themes of the reading and ideas for each lesson.

3. Read through the Scripture passage once, underlining or noting in your Bible anything that stands out to you. Reread the passage again, keeping in mind these three questions: What did you notice, perhaps for the first time? What questions do you have? What did you learn about the heart of God?

4. Write your answers to the questions in this Bible study guide or a notebook. If you do get stuck, first ask God to reveal his Word to you and guide you in his truth. And then, either wait until your small group time or ask a trusted leader for help.

5. Use the end of the lesson to focus your time of prayer, thanking and praising God for the truth of his Word, for what he has revealed to you, and for how he has impacted your daily life.

SUGGESTIONS FOR SMALL GROUP STUDY

The goal of this study is to understand God's Word for you and your community in greater measure, while encountering his heart along the way. A number of practices will help your group as you journey together:

1. Group studies usually go better when everyone is prepared to participate. The best way to prepare is to come having read the lesson's Scripture reading beforehand. Following the suggestions in each individual study will enrich your time as a community as well.

2. Before you begin the study, your group should nominate a leader to guide the discussion. While this person should work through the questions beforehand, his or her main job isn't to lecture, but to

help move the conversation along by asking the lesson questions and facilitating the discussion.

3. Encourage everyone to share. Be sure to listen well, contribute where you feel led, and try not to dominate the conversation.

4. The number one rule for community interaction is: nothing is off-limits! No question is too dumb; no answer is out of bounds. While many questions in this study have "right" answers, most are designed to push you and your friends to explore the passage more deeply and understand what it means for daily living.

5. Finally, be ready for God to reveal himself through the passage being discussed and through the discussion that arises out of the group he's put together. Pray that he would reveal his heart and revelation-light to you all in deeper ways. And be open to being challenged, corrected, and changed.

Again, we pray and trust that this Bible study will kindle in you a burning, passionate desire for God and his heart, while impacting your life for years to come. May it open wide the storehouse of heaven's revelation-light. May it reveal new and greater insights into the mysteries of God and the kingdom-realm life he has for you. And may you encounter the heart of God in more fresh and relevant ways than you ever thought possible!

Introduction to Philippians

What joy and glory came out of Paul's prison cell when he wrote the revelation contained in his letter to the Philippian church. Paul's words point us to heaven! Philippians teaches us how important it is to be joyful throughout the journey of becoming like Christ, and it reveals greater depth on the Person who gives us this joy.

Discover in this, the warmest of Paul's letters, many truths about Jesus Christ—perhaps most significantly, his humiliation and exaltation on high. He left heaven to redeem us and to reveal the heart of God; in this case, the heart of a servant we are called to imitate. Paul also teaches us that our true life is not only in this world, but in the heavenly calling, in the heavenly realm, and in our heavenly life that was given to us through Christ, the heavenly Man. He gave us new birth so that we would be heavenly lights in this dark world as witnesses of Christ's power to change lives. He seated us in the heavenly realm in a place of authority and power. No wonder we should have joy in our hearts!

We've designed this study to help you explore and discover the good and glorious work that Christ has begun in our hearts, which he promises to complete when he is fully unveiled. So read this heavenly letter of joy and be encouraged. And let others know that Jesus is the one who makes every heart sing, flooding us with a bliss that cannot be restrained!

Lesson 1

God's Grace—Gloriously Expressed, Faithfully Completed

PHILIPPIANS 1:1–11

*I'm fully convinced that the One who began this glorious
expression of grace in you will faithfully continue the process of
maturing you through your union with him and will complete it at
the unveiling of our Lord Jesus Christ!*
(Philippians 1:6)

By embarking on this study, you are about to step into heaven's joy, for that's what sits at the heart of this letter. Paul wrote Philippians from the bondage of prison to teach us how important it is to be joyful throughout our journey of becoming like Christ. He offered the joyous revelation-truth that Abba Father will faithfully complete the glorious expression of grace that he began in us.

Think about this. God began the love-mission of his expression of grace by saving you. But that was only step one. In step two, God faithfully continues his expression of grace by breathing new life into every bone in your body until the return of Jesus!

On our road from salvation to maturity in Christ, we receive what Paul speaks of in today's lesson: overflowing love, spiritual insight, and a rich revelation-understanding of God's ways. All so we will be filled to the brim with "the fruits of righteousness that are found in Jesus" and enabled to choose "the most excellent way of all" (1:10-11)—the way of Jesus.

Discover the Heart of God

- After reading Philippians 1:1–11, what did you notice, perhaps for the first time? What questions do you have? What did you learn about the heart of God?

- What was Paul convinced would happen in the lives of the Philippian believers?

- When will God complete the "glorious expression of grace" (1:6) he began in us?

- Why was Paul "in chains"? How did the Philippian believers react to his imprisonment?

- What enables us to choose "the most excellent way of all" (1:10)?

Explore the Heart of God

- Why was it important that Paul identified himself and his coworker as "servants of Jesus, the Anointed One" (1:1)?

- Paul uses language in 1:6 that sounds similar to Genesis 1:31. When God created the heavens and the earth, he declared them to be good. Now, with this new creation life within us, God again sees our growth in his "glorious expression of grace" as something good. What do you think this reveals about the heart of God toward us?

- What does it tell us about the Philippian believers that they remained partners with Paul and Timothy in the wonderful grace of God even though Paul was in chains—a Roman prisoner under guard?

- How does growth in love lead to growth in the knowledge of God?

- How does increasing spiritual insight and knowledge of God enable us to choose the most excellent way of all? What is that way? What does it lead to, and what's the result?

Experience the Heart of God

- Have you ever partnered with other believers for the sake of the gospel? If so, describe that experience. If not, with whom might you be able to develop such a relationship?

• How does it make you feel to know that "the One who began this glorious expression of grace in you will faithfully continue the process of maturing you through your union with him and will complete it at the unveiling of our Lord Jesus Christ!" (1:6)? How does this reveal the heart of God for you?

• Who in your life has risked much, like Paul, so you could experience the heart of God? Who partnered with them to give you that experience?

• How might it look for your love to "grow and increase more and more until it overflows, bringing you into the rich revelation of spiritual insight in all things" (1:9) so that you can experience the heart of God more fully?

- The Greek word translated "choose" (*dokimazo*) in 1:10 means "to examine, to discern, or approve after testing." It comes from a root word that means "accepted" or "pleasing." So discernment becomes the path to finding what God approves, not simply what God forbids. What are some practical steps you can take to choose "the most excellent way of all"?

Share the Heart of God

- Paul and Timothy considered themselves to be servants of Jesus Christ for the sake of others. How would it look to adopt the same outlook and posture yourself in order to share the heart of God?

- How might sharing Philippians 1:6 with people you know encourage them and help them better understand God's heart for them?

• Partnering with others who risk much is crucial for advancing the gospel. How might you partner with others in order to risk much by sharing the heart of God? What kinds of risks might you need to take?

• Who in your life can you pray for, as Paul did for the Philippian Christians—that their love would grow, that they would be brought into the rich revelation of spiritual insight, that they would know God fully, and that they would choose the most excellent way?

CONSIDER THIS

The Christian life is like our natural life: we're born, we grow, we mature. From the day we're reborn in Christ, we follow a similar path. The road from salvation to sanctification is a long and winding one. Sometimes we soar high as we live for Christ. Sometimes we descend into the darkest valley. Regardless, we're promised that no matter what, God will finish what he started!

Lesson 2

———

Our Chaos, God's Gospel Good

PHILIPPIANS 1:12–18

I want you to know, dear ones, what has happened to me has not hindered, but helped my ministry of preaching the gospel, causing it to expand and spread to many people.
(Philippians 1:12)

Sometimes when life takes an unexpected turn for the worse, it can be easy to fixate on our problems and forget the broader picture of God's grand design—for our life and for others. And yet, what we learn in this lesson is that our chaos can be God's gospel good!

Take Paul's life experiences as Exhibit A. At the time he wrote Philippians, he was imprisoned under Roman Praetorian guards. These weren't just any guards; they were the Navy SEALs of the Roman empire. Any one of us might have complained about such treatment—especially while doing God's work. Not Paul. What happened to him didn't matter. All that mattered was what happened for the gospel; even when other ministers were competing with him out of jealousy and impure motives, it just didn't matter.

Paul reiterates in this lesson the same encouragement he shared in Romans: "Every detail of our lives is continually woven together to fit into God's perfect plan of bringing good into our lives" (Romans 8:28). That doesn't mean God causes our painful and chaotic experiences. He can and does use them, though. Both for our good and for God's good—his *gospel* good!

Discover the Heart of God

- After reading Philippians 1:12–18, what did you notice, perhaps for the first time? What questions do you have? What did you learn about the heart of God?

- What did Paul say was the result of his imprisonment?

- Who recognized that Paul was imprisoned for his love of the Anointed One? How had his situation impacted believers throughout the region?

- Paul revealed something surprising about the motives of some who were preaching Christ in the city of Philippi. What did he reveal?

- Paul then revealed that others preached Christ with different motives than the first group had. What were those motives and why did they have them? In spite of these differing motives, why was Paul "overjoyed"?

Explore the Heart of God

- Despite Paul's imprisonment, the gospel went forth and his ministry was fruitful. What does this say about the heart of God and his use of our circumstances for his glory?

- How can our personal struggles and difficult situations encourage other believers' lives and work for God's gospel good?

- Paul exposed two ministry groups with competing sets of motivations for preaching Christ. What do you think fed these different motivations? Where did they come from? How do we guard against negative motives and cultivate positive ones?

- Why is it true what Paul said, that as long as Christ is preached we can rejoice, regardless of the motivations of others?

Experience the Heart of God

- What should we learn from Paul's experience of the heart of God in the midst of his incredible circumstances?

- Consider your own difficult life situations. How might God want to use them to advance his gospel and encourage other believers to boldly bear witness to the Word of God?

- Have you known people who have preached Christ out of less than pure motives? In light of 1:17–18, how can you respond?

Share the Heart of God

- Paul clearly believed that his own difficulties wouldn't get in the way of Christ being preached. How can you ensure that your own hardships don't hinder God's heart from being shared?

- Despite Paul's imprisonment, his testimony of the love of Christ shone bright and strong—even before his enemies! How can you share the same love with those who mistreat you so that you can lead them to God's heart?

- How do your motivations in sharing the heart of God compare with 1:15–16? Do you share out of "competition and controversy" or with "grace and love"?

CONSIDER THIS

One of the consistent themes of Scripture is that when life turns ugly, God is still good! Consider the story of Joseph in the book of Genesis. His brothers intended to harm him, but God used it for good to accomplish the saving of many people. The same was true for Paul. The same is true for us. The chaos of our lives can be used for God's gospel good. Always!

Lesson 3

Christ Made Manifest, in Life or Death

PHILIPPIANS 1:19–30

No matter what, I will continue to preach and
hold tightly to Christ, so that he will be openly revealed
through me before everyone's eyes...In my life or in my death,
Christ will be manifested in me.
(Philippians 1:20)

How someone lives says a lot about a person—how they spend their time, where they spend their money, what they pursue and dream about. The same could be said about how people die. Do they live out the final years of their lives pointing to themselves or to others? Do they give up or fight to the end? Do they have hope or despair about what's to come?

Paul wrestled with similar questions. He was torn between whether he should go on living despite a hope for heaven and eternal life with Christ awaiting him. And who could blame him? In another letter Paul wrote, he revealed how he had suffered—through beatings and lashings, being ship-wrecked and abandoned, experiencing hunger and homelessness. It makes sense that Paul longed to be liberated from this life.

Paul determined that no matter what, he would live well and end well. Whatever happened to him, whether in life or death, he wanted Christ to be magnified. May we join Paul in never giving up, continuing to live our lives based on the reality of Christ's gospel, and fighting together until the very end!

Discover the Heart of God

- After reading Philippians 1:19–30, what did you notice, perhaps for the first time? What questions do you have? What did you learn about the heart of God?

- Why did Paul believe he would be delivered from his hardship and spared? No matter what happened to him, what did Paul say he would continue to do? Why?

- What was the dilemma Paul faced as he lived imprisoned and continued in ministry? Why did he declare he wouldn't be "ashamed" (1:20)?

- What did Paul urge the Christians in Philippi to do that was more important than worrying about his situation?

- What did Paul say would be the result when the Philippian believers stood united in one spirit and one passion?

Explore the Heart of God

- Paul said in 1:19 that he would be delivered because of the lavish supply of Jesus' Spirit and the Philippian believers' intercession for him. How are these two connected?

- How is it that Christ was revealed through Paul's preaching of Christ and his holding on to him? How is it that in both Paul's life and his death Christ was manifest?

- The Greek word for "liberated" in 1:22–24 is a word sailors used, meaning for them to "loose the ship and set sail." For farmers, the word meant "to unyoke an oxen (set it free)." Why is this passage about being "liberated" from this life such a dilemma for Paul and for every believer? What does it reveal about what happens to us when we die?

- How does it look to continue living "based on the reality of the gospel of Christ" (1:27), no matter what happens in life?

- Why does unity provide such a strong, sure defense against opposition? How does such communal courage "prove as a sure sign from God of their coming destruction" (1:28)?

- Paul said that he and the Philippian Christians were "in this fight together until we win the prize" (1:30). What is the prize Paul was referencing?

Experience the Heart of God

- Think of a time when you experienced the heart of God through both the "lavish supply of the Spirit of Jesus" and others interceding to God on your behalf. Describe that experience.

- In 1:20, Paul said he passionately clung to Christ. The Greek word is *apokaradokia* and can be translated "with the deepest and intense yearnings" or "with the concentrated desire that abandons all other interests with outstretched hands in expectation." How might it look in your own life to reflect Paul's determination to abandon all other interests by holding tightly to Christ?

- In 1:21, Paul said, "My true life is the Anointed One, and dying means gaining more of him." Do you think of your life in this way? Do you share Paul's dilemma? Explain.

- How might it look to live your life based on the reality of the gospel of Christ? How would living this way deepen your experience of the heart of God?

- Have you ever suffered for Christ? If so, what was that like? If not, how might it look in your life to take seriously the struggle Paul spoke of in 1:28–30?

Share the Heart of God

- Paul believed his deliverance would come through both the power of Christ and the prayers of believers. For whom can you intercede so they can experience the heart of God through deliverance?

- Paul believed that every day of life afforded him the opportunity to bear more fruit in ministry. Paul was excited to help the Philippians make pioneer advances in their faith and joy. How can you adopt the same mind-set as you share the heart of God?

- Describe what it means and how it looks for believers to "stand united in one Spirit and one passion" (1:27) for the sake of sharing the heart of God?

- Why is suffering for Christ actually an opportunity to not only experience the heart of God in increasing measure but also to share it?

CONSIDER THIS

"Whatever happens," Paul said, "keep living your lives based on the reality of the gospel of Christ" (1:27). How are you living your life? Is Christ made manifest in you, whether in life or death? Does he shine through when times are good and bad—so that he's revealed to others?

Lesson 4

Let Jesus' Mind-Set Become Your Motivation

PHILIPPIANS 2:1-11

Consider the example that Jesus, the Anointed One,
has set before us. Let his mindset become your motivation.
(Philippians 2:5)

In the last lesson we saw how Paul wrestled with a dilemma. He longed to be fully joined with Christ, which would happen at death, yet he also recognized that the longer he lived, the more fruit he would bear for the sake of the gospel. That's quite a dilemma! Paul invites us to do what he did: keep living our lives based on Christ's gospel reality.

Paul's invitation highlights a crucial question for our gospel-driven lives: what's our motivation for living? Clearly Paul's motivation wasn't about living a life of luxury. It wasn't about climbing the corporate ladder and "making it." It wasn't a motivation to "eat, drink, and be merry," as the world often trumpets. Paul didn't want to continue living for his own sake; he was motivated to serve others.

What drove his motivation? The mind-set of Christ! Jesus' example of self-emptying—renouncing the advantages of his deity, relinquishing his right to life itself—set the course for how Paul would live. In this lesson Paul turns our attention toward that example. May it motivate us to joyously empty ourselves for the sake of the world.

Discover the Heart of God

- After reading Philippians 2:1–11, what did you notice, perhaps for the first time? What questions do you have? What did you learn about the heart of God?

- What are some benefits believers have in their relationship with Jesus?

38

- Why did Paul instruct the Philippian believers to be free from controversial or prideful opinions? What did he want from them instead of self-promotion?

- What example and mind-set did Paul want the Philippian believers to consider to help shape their motivations?

- Despite the reality that Jesus was God, he laid aside the advantages of his deity to become a man. What else did he do in laying aside those advantages? List everything from 2:6–8.

- Why did God exalt Christ? What did he give him? How will everything and everyone, one day, respond to Christ?

Explore the Heart of God

- Explain how each of the marks of unity—one heart, one passion, one love—should manifest themselves in local churches and also in the global church?

- How do "pride-filled opinions" hinder and harm unity? Why should believers consider the example of Jesus? What's so important about letting his mind-set become our motivation?

- Why is it so important to the Christian faith that Jesus really is God, as Paul revealed in 2:6? What did Paul mean when he said that Jesus "emptied himself of his outward glory" (2:7)? In what way was Jesus obedient to his Father and the perfect example for us?

- Notice the seven steps Christ took from the throne to the cross in verses 7–8: 1) he emptied himself; 2) he became a servant; 3) he became human; 4) he humbled himself; 5) he became vulnerable and revealed as a man; 6) he was obedient until his death; 7) he died a criminal's death on the cross. What does this reveal about the heart of God? How should it affect our motivation for loving service?

- Why does it matter and why is it significant that Jesus has been exalted, that he's been given the greatest name of all, and that he will be submitted to by everything and everyone?

Experience the Heart of God

- How have you found strength and encouragement in your experience of the heart of God in relation with Jesus?

- Have you ever experienced the power of Christian unity, when believers walk together in harmonious purpose? What about the fallout that comes from disunity? How have either influenced your experience of the heart of God?

- How should Jesus' example of self-emptying, service, obedience, and humiliation impact your daily life? What might his example mean for your experience of the heart of God?

- Paul revealed in this passage that Christ has all authority and reigns supreme. So much so that "every tongue will proclaim in every language" that Jesus is Lord (2:11). Are you submitting to Jesus as Lord and God?

Share the Heart of God

- Look at what believers receive from their relationship with Jesus in 2:1. Whom do you know who would welcome what Christ offers if you shared the heart of God with them?

- How can being joined together with other believers in "one heart, one passion, and united in one love" (2:2) help you share the heart of God?

- Read 2:3–4 again. Why are these instructions so crucial for sharing the heart of God with those you know?

- How might it look in your life if you "let [Jesus'] mind-set become your motivation," as Paul outlined in 2:5–8? How would it impact the way you share of the heart of God?

CONSIDER THIS

Remarkably, the one through whom, by whom, and for whom the universe was made chose to empty himself of his outward glory! He did this by humbly becoming a human, giving up all self-promotion and selfishness—to the point of dying as a lowly servant. Jesus is our example for how we are to live and love. May his mind-set become your motivation as you experience and share the heart of God.

Lesson 5

Live a Joy-Filled, Faithful Life

PHILIPPIANS 2:12–30

*Live a cheerful life, without complaining or division
among yourselves. For then you will be seen as innocent,
faultless, and pure children of God. (Philippians 2:14-15)*

We live in depressing times: bomb blasts, the plunging stock market, political scandals, and business closings. They've become part of the daily background noise that drums in our ears, on top of all the other things that disrupt our lives. And yet Paul has a word for us in these troubled times: don't complain, don't quarrel, and live a life of cheer.

In today's lesson, Paul charges us with the task of joy-filled, faithful living for a purpose—a gospel-driven purpose. He wants us to live a cheerful life so that we will shine like stars amid our dark, perverse culture. Such living—the joy-filled, faithful life of heaven—reveals us as innocent, faultless, pure children of God before the eyes of the world. This kind of living is also the way we can offer those around us the words of eternal life.

Paul points us to two people who lived the kind of life he calls us to:

Timothy and Epaphroditus. These two joyously served those entrusted to them and faithfully acted as ministers of the gospel.

So listen to Paul: "Live a cheerful life, without complaining or division among yourselves" (2:14).

Discover the Heart of God

- After reading Philippians 2:12–30, what did you notice, perhaps for the first time? What questions do you have? What did you learn about the heart of God?

- In light of the fact that the Philippian believers had always listened to Paul, what more did he ask of them?

• How did Paul instruct believers to live? Why? What will be the result?

• Even though believers "live in the midst of a brutal and perverse culture" (2:15), what will happen when they live as God's children are called to live? What did Paul say God will do for believers who make their new life manifested as they live?

• Why did Paul say Timothy "is like no other" (2:20)? Why did he ask the Philippian believers to welcome Epaphroditus?

Explore the Heart of God

- What did Paul mean when he told the believers to "make this new life fully manifested as you live in the holy awe of God" (2:12)? How do we do that?

- Why did Paul instruct believers to "live a cheerful life" (2:14)? What purpose does it serve?

- Why were the Philippian believers living proof that Paul hadn't labored among them for nothing? Why did this matter to Paul?

- Why did Paul say he "will rejoice in ecstatic celebration and triumph with all of you" (2:17), even if he lost his life or shed his blood?

- What do the behavior and reputations of Timothy and Epaphroditus reveal about the heart of God, especially when it comes to ministry?

Experience the Heart of God

- Many of us have, at one point in our lives, had someone mentor and instruct us in the Christian faith. Who was that for you? How can you keep following this person's guidance and instructions as if he or she were right there with you, so you can experience the heart of God more deeply?

- Paul said we are called to make the new life of Christ "fully manifested." In what ways is it *not* fully realized in your life? How might it look to manifest it fully as you live in the holy awe of God?

- Paul said people like Epaphroditus desire to be welcomed "with joyous love" (2:29). Whom do you know who serves as a minister of the Lord, and how can you welcome and serve him or her in the same way?

Share the Heart of God

- It's no surprise that we Christians live as the Philippians did: in a "brutal and perverse culture." How can we shine as lights, sharing the heart of God by "offering them the words of eternal life" (2:15–16)?

- Many of us have had the privilege of guiding others in the Christian life. Who is the fruit of your own ministry? With whom have you shared the heart of God, so that you too can boast at the unveiling of Christ upon his return?

- Read again Paul's testimony about Timothy and Epaphroditus in 2:19–26. How could you model your life after them, earn a similar reputation, and share God's heart for the sake of God's glory?

CONSIDER THIS

Every day we're pressed in on every side by bad global news and bad personal news. Yet we're called to make our new life in Christ "fully manifested as [we] live in the holy awe of God." How? By living a life of cheer! And that's a tall order. Thankfully, we're not on our own in this, because, as Paul promised: "God will continually revitalize you, implanting within you the passion" to live this cheerful life" (2:13).

Lesson 6

Die with Christ to Live Again

PHILIPPIANS 3:1–11

*I will be one with him in his sufferings and I will be one
with him in his death. Only then will I be able to
experience complete oneness with him in his resurrection
from the realm of death.* (Philippians 3:10–11)

Today's lesson is a countercultural statement if there ever was one. Boasting in our own strengths is common today. Holding on to our lives— who we are, all of our accomplishments, what we desire to acquire and gain—is thought to be the only way to get ahead and enjoy power. Not so for Paul!

Of all people, Paul had the right to boast in who he was and how he lived, especially when it came to being made right with God. Yet he came to a point in his spiritual journey where he realized that his accolades weren't useful for anything but the garbage heap. Of course this mirrors Jesus' own teaching: "All who seek to live apart from me will lose it all. But those who let go of their lives for my sake and surrender it all to me will discover true life!" (Matthew 10:39).

What we discover in today's lesson is this: only in letting go of our accomplishments and claims to earned righteousness will we find what we've been looking for—the power of Jesus' resurrection working in us.

Discover the Heart of God

- After reading Philippians 3:1–11, what did you notice, perhaps for the first time? What questions do you have? What did you learn about the heart of God?

- In whom did Paul say we should boast? In whom shouldn't we boast?

- Paul said that he had relied on a number of things from his personal background and achievements to impress people and become right with God. List them."

- What did Paul say he thought of his accomplishments in light of "the delight of experiencing Jesus Christ as my Lord!" (3:7)?

- What was Paul's passion? What did he long to know and experience?

Explore the Heart of God

- Why did Paul warn the Philippian Christians to beware of "religious hypocrites"? Who were they, what were they teaching, and where else did Paul address them?

- Paul said we don't have to worry about pleasing God through circumcision because we've "experienced 'heart-circumcision'" (3:3). What does this mean?

- Based on Paul's list of accomplishments in 3:4–6, why did he have reason to boast? Why were they now like "a pile of manure" (3:8)?

- According to Paul, what does it mean to "know" Jesus Christ? What does this entail?

- In 3:10-11, Paul linked himself with Christ's suffering, dying, and rising. Why? How is being one with Christ in his sufferings and death necessary to being one with him in his resurrection?

Experience the Heart of God

- How might it look, practically, to never "limit [our] joy or fail to rejoice in the wonderful experience of knowing our Lord Jesus" (3:1)?

- It can be hard to fully lean into the reality that we serve and worship God "in the power and freedom of the Holy Spirit, not in laws and religious duties" (3:3). Do you find yourself trying to please God through laws and religious duty, rather than the power and freedom of his Spirit? How might that impact your experience of the heart of God?

- Paul realized that, compared to the surpassing greatness of knowing Christ and intimately experiencing him, who he was and what he did in his own strength was worthless. Write a list about yourself similar to what Paul did in 3:4–6. What personal boastings do you need to throw "on the garbage heap" (3:8)?

- At the end of our reading, Paul made a profound statement: it's only in suffering and dying with Christ—to self and sin—that we can rise to new life with him. What do you need to suffer through and die to in order to fully experience the resurrection heart of God?

Share the Heart of God

- How might limiting your joy, or failing to rejoice in your wonderful experience with Jesus, impact how you share the heart of God?

- Why is it such good news for people you know that we serve God through the power and freedom of his Spirit, rather than through laws and religious duty?

• What are some things people boast about to try to make themselves righteous or to try to please God? How might sharing the ideas from this lesson be important to their spiritual journey?

• To a culture that says things like "Obey Your Thirst" and "Be Your Way," the idea of dying to self doesn't set well. Yet this perspective leads to death! Why is it important to share this aspect of the heart of God? How might you go about doing it?

CONSIDER THIS

Phrases like "Obey Your Thirst" and "Be Your Way" are more than corporate taglines. For many people, these slogans are mottos for living. And yet, Christ calls us to die to ourselves—our accomplishments and agendas, our religious works and righteous claims—in order to rise to new life with him. May Paul's passion be your passion: be consumed with Christ, not clinging to your own "righteousness."

Lesson 7

Forget Your Past, Fasten Your Heart to the Future

PHILIPPIANS 3:12-21

I do have one compelling focus: I forget all of the past as
I fasten my heart to the future instead. I run straight for the
divine invitation of reaching the heavenly goal and
gaining the victory-prize through the anointing of Jesus.
(Philippians 3:13–14)

Forgetting our past, fastening our hearts to the future—easier said than done. But that's the focus of today's lesson. When you realize the person who gave this advice was the apostle Paul, that makes it even more profound. There are two reasons for this.

First, Paul declared that in his pursuit of Christ, he forgot what was in his past. Part of that past was his religious zeal and pursuit of God's righteousness through religious works. Another part was his acts to destroy the church. Through the joy of the Spirit, Paul was able to leave behind all of this past striving and shame.

Second, we're reminded that none of us has arrived. Not even Paul!

Paul wanted to know Christ more intimately by experiencing Jesus' full resurrection power. But he admitted that he hadn't yet acquired this. Acquiring "absolute fullness" and oneness with Christ in his resurrection was something Paul looked forward to in the future. So he fastened his heart to that singular focus.

This lesson is about both forgetting and fastening. May we join Paul in forgetting all of what's in the past—both our mistakes and our achievements—and fastening our hearts to the glorious future that awaits us in Christ!

Discover the Heart of God

- After reading Philippians 3:12–21, what did you notice, perhaps for the first time? What questions do you have? What did you learn about the heart of God?

- What did Paul say he had not yet acquired? Though he hadn't fully attained his goal, what did he do to achieve it? What was his ultimate goal?

- What was Paul's "one compelling focus" (3:13)? What was he running straight toward?

- What did Paul say he wanted for those who were fully mature? If they didn't have it, what did he say would happen?

- How did Paul describe those who "live by different standards" than the true way of God?

Explore the Heart of God

- What did Paul mean that he hadn't "yet acquired the absolute fullness that I'm pursuing" (3:12)? Why hadn't he? Is this surprising to you?

- Why was Paul able to "forget all of the past" and "fasten [his] heart to the future instead" (3:13)? What does this tell us about the heart of God?

- Ultimately, what was it that Paul was running to achieve? Why should we have the same goal?

• What did Paul mean when he said that we are "a colony of heaven on earth" (3:20)?

• How is it that the Lord Jesus Christ transforms and transfigures us? How does this look, and when does it take place?

Experience the Heart of God

• How does it make you feel knowing a Christian titan like Paul hadn't yet acquired the fullness of his faith's pursuit? How should this encourage your own experience and pursuit of the heart of God?

- Paul said he didn't depend on his own strength to achieve victory in his faith, yet it's so easy to do that. In what ways do Christians depend on their own power over the Holy Spirit's in their spiritual journeys? In what ways might you be doing this?

- Paul encouraged the Philippian believers to imitate his walk with God. Who can you imitate as you run the race in pursuit of the heart of God?

- Paul said that there are those inside and outside the church who pursue different standards than Christ. Have you witnessed this yourself? How can you guard against these different standards?

- How do you think it looks to fully live out our identity and calling as a colony of heaven on earth? Why must we "cling tightly to our Life-Giver" as we live out this identity?

Share the Heart of God

- Sometimes people get so weary of running the "Christian life" race. Yet 3:12–16 offers hope! How would sharing the heart of God found in these verses be an encouragement to those you know?

- One of the points Paul makes is that the Christian journey isn't a solo trek. Instead, we need to "advance together to reach this victory-prize" (3:16). Whom do you know who needs help running the race in order to fully experience the victory-prize: the heart of God?

- While it may seem like a tall order, modeling how it looks and what it means to live for Christ is an effective way to share the heart of God with people. How can you live in such a way that others could imitate your walk in pursuit of the prize?

CONSIDER THIS

Most of us long for the future, but we often focus on the past. In Christ, we don't have to! Like a runner straining for the finish line, we can look forward to our future hope in Christ without looking back. So keep your eyes fixed on Jesus, "who birthed faith within us and who leads us forward into faith's perfection" (Hebrews 12:2).

Lesson 8

———

Always Be Cheerful with Joyous Celebration

PHILIPPIANS 4:1–23

Be cheerful with joyous celebration in every season of life.
Let joy overflow, for you are united with the Anointed One!
(Philippians 4:4)

In the late '80s and early '90s, there was a popular saying that could summarize today's lesson: *Don't worry, be happy.* Paul has a similar message for us as he ends his letter, but it goes deeper than a detached philosophy of denial: "Celebrate with cheer and joy in every season of life. and don't be anxious about anything!"

Paul ends our journey through this heavenly letter by drawing our attention to the *source* of our joy: our Anointed One. Why should we be cheerful at every turn? Because we've been united with Christ's very life! And when life does turn sour, we don't have to worry in isolation. We can bring our anxiety over math tests and health tests, new jobs and job cuts, debt and divorce before God's very throne— "with overflowing gratitude" (4:6). When we do, Paul promises that God's peace will provide all the answers we need.

Paul's own "don't worry, be happy" encouragement isn't just a fatalistic shoulder shrug. No, he learned the secret to having real joy and satisfaction in everything. May we listen with attentive hearts to what he has to share.

Discover the Heart of God

- After reading Philippians 4:1-23, what did you notice, perhaps for the first time? What questions do you have? What did you learn about the heart of God?

- Paul had some words for two women, Euodias and Syntyche. What were those words? Who else did he address, and why?

- Instead of being pulled in different directions by our emotions or worries about life, what did Paul say we should do? How should we do it?

- What did Paul promise God will do when we tell him every detail of our lives?

- What gave Paul the strength that enabled him to conquer every difficulty?

Explore the Heart of God

- Relational conflict is found in every church. Paul encouraged two dear women in this congregation, Euodias and Syntyche, to resolve all of their disagreements. These names give us a clue. Euodias means "a fair journey." Syntyche can mean "an accident." Along our faith journey, we may collide with one another, but God always has grace for restoration. How did Paul's desire for these women to resolve their issues reflect the heart of God?

- Why is it important for us to be cheerful and joyous in every season of life? Why don't we have to worry about anything during these seasons?

- Why should every believer be "saturated in prayer throughout each day" (4:6)? How do you think it looks to live in this way?

- In 4:8, Paul listed a number of things believers should be continually fixing their minds on. Why is this list so important to our Christian life? How do each of them shape that life?

- Paul said he had "learned to be satisfied and undisturbed in any circumstance" (4:11). Why could he say this? Are you as convinced as Paul that "God will fully satisfy every need you have" (4:19)?

Experience the Heart of God

- Has anyone ever become your "glorious joy and crown of reward" because of your ministry in his or her life? Who was it, and how did that happen?

- Paul relates the resolution of Euodias and Syntyche's disagreement and division to the theme of Christian unity. Is there anyone with whom you need to be restored in order to maintain "one mind in our Lord"?

- When did you experience a difficult season of life? Did you respond with joy and cheer? If so, how hard was it to have this mind-set? If not, how might having this mind-set have helped your circumstances and your experience of the heart of God?

- Describe when you experienced the power of prayer and the peace of God during a difficult time. What was that experience of God's heart like?

- Satisfaction in life seems hard to come by, yet Paul found it. Have you? If so, how? If not, what do you think it would take to be satisfied in all things?

Share the Heart of God

- Helping to restore brothers and sisters to unity in Christ is one way we can share the heart of God. Consider again the story of Euodias and Syntyche in 4:2–3. Do you know of relationships you could help restore, as Paul asked Syzygos to do for these women?

- Being cheerful with joyous celebration isn't easy when life takes a turn for the worse. How might such an attitude help you share the heart of God with those you know?

- We all know people who need prayer. They are part of the faith-filled requests we bring before God. Spend time telling God the details of those in your life who need what he offers in 4:7.

- Paul revealed how pivotal the Philippian Christians were financially for his ministry. Whom do you know or what ministry are you aware of where you can sow seeds of financial support?

CONSIDER THIS

"Don't worry, be happy" may be a secular slogan of detachment from the cares of this life, but it's a pretty good way to summarize Philippians. This letter unleashes upon the church heaven's joy, which melts away our worries and infuses us with hope-filled happiness. In closing, remember these words of Paul: "I am convinced that my God will fully satisfy every need you have, for I have seen the abundant riches of glory revealed to me through the Anointed One, Jesus Christ!" (4:19).

Encounter the Heart of God

The Passion Translation Bible is a new, heart-level translation that expresses God's fiery heart of love to this generation, using Hebrew, Greek, and Aramaic manuscripts and merging the emotion and life-changing truth of God's Word. If you are hungry for God and want to know him on a deeper level, The Passion Translation will help you encounter God's heart and discover what he has for your life.

The Passion Translation box set includes the following eight books:

Psalms: Poetry on Fire

Proverbs: Wisdom from Above

Song of Songs: Divine Romance

Matthew: Our Loving King

John: Eternal Love

Luke and Acts: To the Lovers of God

Hebrews and James: Faith Works

Letters from Heaven: From the Apostle Paul (Galatians, Ephesians, Philippians, Colossians, I & II Timothy)

Additional titles available include:

Mark: Miracles and Mercy
Romans: Grace and Glory
1 & 2 Corinthians: Love and Truth
Letters of Love: From Peter, John, and Jude (1, 2 Peter; 1, 2, 3 John; Jude)

THE
PASSION
TRANSLATION

thePassionTranslation.com

thePassionTranslation.com